D0903155

Having a
Disability

by Louise Spilsbury

illustrated by Ximena Jeria

PICTURE WINDOW BOOKS
a capstone imprint

Questions and Feelings About . . . is published by
Picture Window Books, a Capstone imprint
1710 Roe Crest Drive, North Mankato, MN 56003
www.mycapstone.com

Library of Congress Cataloging-in-Publication Data is available on
the Library of Congress website.

ISBN: 978-1-5158-4543-0 (library binding)

Editor: Melanie Palmer
Design: Lisa Peacock
Author: Louise Spilsbury
Consultant: Barbara Band

First published in Great Britain in 2018
by The Watts Publishing Group
Copyright © The Watts Publishing Group, 2018
All rights reserved.

Printed and bound in China.
001593

Having a
Disability

Everyone has different abilities.
We're all good at different things.

Some people like to dance and sing. Other people like to write stories, make models, or bake cakes.

What are you good at?

We all have things that we find hard to do as well.
When someone has a disability there are lots
of things they can do, but there are some things
they find hard to do.

What things do you find hard?

There are different kinds of disabilities.
Some children are born with a disability.

Some people are born with only one arm or one leg.
This is called a physical disability. They may be given
a plastic arm or leg.

Some children have a disability after they were very ill or because they had a bad accident. This kind of disability may last a short time, or it could last for their whole life.

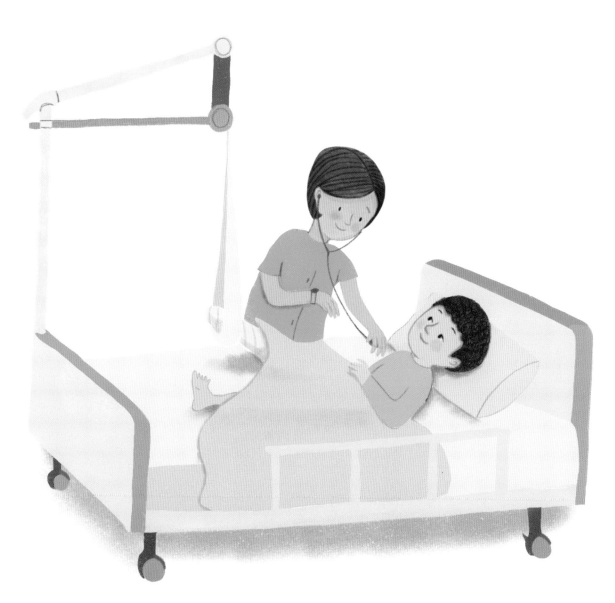

If you have a disability you may use tools to help you do things more easily. Tools are objects or machines that help us.

Everyone needs tools to help them do various tasks.

What tools help you to do things?

Some people use their legs to help them move around.
Other people need to use a wheelchair.

We all get around in our own way. The only thing that matters is that we get where we want to go!

Some people have a visual disability and are blind or cannot see very well. They can use a white stick to help them find their way.

This also shows other people that they cannot see very well.

Some children cannot hear very well and wear a hearing aid in their ear. It makes sounds louder and clearer so they can hear better.

Some people use sign language for words instead of sounds.

Do you know any sign language?

19

Disabilities can affect the way people learn.
We all learn things in different ways and
at different speeds.

Sometimes we need a little extra help to make learning easier or faster.

Which subjects do you need help with?

Some people find listening or sitting quietly
very hard and cannot concentrate for very long.

But they are very good at other things,
like running fast or using computers.

When we have a friend who is different from us, we might want to ask about their differences. It's interesting to learn about the ways that we are all different.

We can all learn a lot from each other.

What makes you different?

When we find out what people like and what they can do, we don't have to guess. When we guess, we might make mistakes. If we guess someone cannot play a game when they really can, they might feel left out.

How do you feel if you're left out of a game?

When we get to know people we find that
we are more alike than we are different.
We often like the same food, films,
sports, or games!

We all deserve the chance to learn, play, and be happy together. We should be proud of the ways we are different and of the things we have in common.

And we should all focus on what we can do,
especially when we work together!

Notes for Caregivers

This book can be a useful guide for families and professionals to discuss the many different aspects of disability, to aid communication, and to help promote discussion, enabling children to express their thoughts and feelings. It also encourages a broader understanding of the world around them.

Handling disability can be overwhelming. Over time everyone adjusts to living in a different way, but it can be a challenging time. Everyone reacts and copes in a different way. Children may feel much more self-conscious. It is important that everyone has someone to talk to about how they feel.

Select appropriate vocabulary when discussing disabilities. Many myths and misleading terms can be debunked. Everyone is different. Having a disability is one of those differences, but people are not defined by their disability. Difference is part of our individual uniqueness. Acceptance and tolerance of differences is important to learn at an early age. We can draw on what we have in common as well as what is different about us. Choosing some activities that focus on participation and being inclusive will help to bridge any physical differences in a class or group.

Group Activities

1. You can help all children understand what it feels like to have a disability by creating a few role-play situations, such as covering eyes or ears, using crutches, or using a wheelchair. Discuss what tasks became harder or what senses the children had to rely on.

2. Hold a session on sign language or lip reading, which can provide a good opportunity for developing communication skills.

3. Think about everyday tools that help us and how they can be adapted for disabled people. Talk about the different equipment such as a ramp or lift for a wheelchair. What other examples do the children know about?

4. Discuss famous people who have overcome disability or achieved their dream. Helen Keller, Beethoven, Stephen Hawking, and Frieda Kahlo are some examples.

Read More:

Burcaw, Shane. *Not So Different*. Roaring Brook Press, 2017.

Reeves, Alice. *Roxy the Raccoon: A Story to Help Children Learn about Disability and Inclusion*. Jessica Kingsley Publishers, 2018.

Willis, Jeanne. *Susan Laughs*. Henry Holt and Co., 2000.

Read the entire Questions and Feelings About . . . series:

Adoption
Autism
Bullying
Having a Disability
Racism
When Parents Separate
When Someone Dies
Worries